A Month at the Front

# A Month at the Front
*The Diary of an Unknown Soldier*

BODLEIAN LIBRARY
UNIVERSITY OF OXFORD

First published in 2006 by the Bodleian Library
Broad Street
Oxford OX1 3BG

www.bodleianbookshop.co.uk

Reprinted in 2014

ISBN 978 185124 422 5

Designed by Dot Little.
Printed and bound by TJ International Ltd, Padstow, Cornwall
British Library Catalogue in Publishing Data
A CIP record of this publication is available from the British Library

The small black notebook which contains the manuscript of *A Month at the Front* (originally entitled *A Month's Experiences at the Front*) came to the Bodleian in the summer of 2005 as part of a much larger donation of unrelated material. The donor had no knowledge of its provenance or past history.

At first sight unremarkable, examination of the notebook showed that it contained a hand-written journal covering approximately one month in the summer of 1917, detailing the experiences of a group of British soldiers as they moved up to the front and then took part in an assault on the German lines. No exact dates or place names were given, but a clue was provided by the presence of two photographs showing the grave of Private A. M. Williams of the East Surrey Regiment in Reninghelst Military Cemetery, and of a letter of condolence to his parents. However, Williams could not be the author of the journal as he is mentioned in it by name; rather it seems as though it was written by one of his friends and comrades, possibly already invalided back to Britain, in order to explain to his family what had happened to him. Its vividness and immediacy suggests that, although not written at the exact time of the events described, it was composed not long afterwards.

Considering the horrors it describes, the style of the journal is remarkably dispassionate, but this very understatement also gives it much of its power. In this, it is very similar to other accounts by 'Tommies' who survived the First World War, most notably to the 1934 documentary film *Forgotten Men*, in which a number of veterans somewhat reluctantly relive their experiences at the prompting of Sir John Hammerton, a well-known popular historian of the time. More recently Richard Holmes has written that the defining characteristics of the First World War soldier were courage and endurance[1], and it is precisely these qualities which shine out from the narrative.

The writer of *A Month at the Front* nowhere reveals his name, but he states at the outset that he was a private soldier in D Company of the 12th Battalion, East Surrey Regiment. This Battalion was formed in the spring of 1915. The war had already lasted for nine months and it was clear that the early expectations of a quick victory were not going to be realized. The original British Expeditionary Force had been destroyed as a fighting force by the battles of 1914, and, despite the success of Kitchener's recruiting campaign which raised an army of half a million men, by the beginning of 1915 the army was again beginning to suffer from acute shortages of manpower.

Thus was born the idea of the 'Pals' battalions, in which groups of friends from the same area could enlist together and serve in the same unit. The idea originated in Lancashire, but was quickly taken up in other parts of the country. The Mayor of Bermondsey received a letter from the War Office requesting that the borough raise a battalion of infantry, and this letter was discussed at a meeting of the council on 4 May 1915. Despite opposition from some members, on the grounds that Bermondsey was already doing its bit as regards recruiting, the scheme was approved, and the Battalion was formed officially on 24 May. The Town Hall, Rotherhithe, became the Battalion's headquarters and main recruiting office, and initial training took place at the Oval, Southwark Park. The Battalion first went overseas to France a year later in May 1916 and took part in the Battle of the Somme.

After the war, the Battalion was the subject of a detailed history by John Aston and L.M. Duggan,[2] and by comparing the narrative of the journal with this and other records of the regiment it is possible to place the text in context.[3]

At the beginning of July 1917, just before the narrative begins, the Battalion was resting at a place called La Roukloshille in Flanders. Although not far from the front line, this was regarded as a quiet place, and the opportunity was taken for reorganisation, refitting, and sport. The latter included an inter-company football tournament, the trophy for which was a barrel of stout. Many of the men also took the opportunity to use the baths ('very welcome' according to John Aston), and some went foraging for peas in the fields of neighbouring farms, an action for which they were later stopped a franc from their pay to make good the damage they had caused.

On 23 July, around the time the journal begins, the Battalion moved from La Roukloshille to Wood Camp, from where they were to proceed to relieve the 8th Battalion, the London Regiment, in the line the following day. Although the fact was kept from the men, they were to take part in the initial assault in the Third Battle of Ypres (Passchendaele), which lasted from 31 July to 6 November, 1917.

On 24 July the Battalion moved up to the line, being allocated a section just south-west of the Ypres-Comines canal, behind the pile of ruins which was all that remained of the 'White Chateau' mentioned in the narrative. The men of D Company were allocated dugouts known as the Bois Confluent and the Old French trench. For the next few days they were employed mainly on working parties, one particularly nasty job being that of salvaging around the White Chateau, as described in the journal. Throughout this period the Germans maintained a heavy bombardment of the British lines, and on the night of the 28th they fired several gas shells into the area where the Battalions headquarters was situated. Difficult and dangerous as these days were, however, they were merely preparatory to the main assault on the German lines, which was planned to start at the end of the month. Accordingly on the 30th the Battalion moved up to its assembly positions, D Company being in a trench called Oblique Row.

The attack, which forms the climax of the journal, began with a massive artillery bombardment at 3.50am on 31 July. According to the plan, the 12th Surreys were meant to remain in a supporting role, the main burden of the attack being borne by the 11th Royal West Kents and the 18$^{th}$ King's Royal Rifles. Their ultimate objective was the village of Hollebeke. However, as so often during the First World War, things turned out very differently from how they had been planned. For this, the weather, as so often during the Passchendaele campaign, was to a large extent responsible. Another member of the 12$^{th}$ East Surreys, Captain David Walker, later wrote:

> July 31$^{st}$ will ever remain a date to be remembered by those who took part in the assault on Hollebeke. It had rained in torrents and without ceasing for some days, and, once the battle had begun and the heavy rains continued, the weather took control of the situation. It is difficult for a reader to imagine the awful expanse of slimy mud just south of the Ypres– Comines canal, which was our Divisional Sector. Our attacking troops plodded on through this until all but beaten by physical exhaustion. Many never rose from the mire.

In addition, the Germans offered strong resistance and the men of the King's Royal Rifles in particular were mown down by machine gun fire as they advanced across no man's land. Lance Corporal H. G. Farrell, another member of D Company, takes up the story:

> Within a few minutes the wounded started coming back. The first man I saw came running back minus his trousers and with a nice 'Blighty' one. Within a short time the trench we were in, which was used as a first dressing station, was packed with wounded. Whether they ran

forward too fast into our barrage (which was a jumping one), or whether 'Jerry' had got the range, I do not know, but it was evident in a very short time that the attack on this sector had failed.

It was thus decided that the 12<sup>th</sup> East Surreys should move forward and take over the attack. Accordingly, at 6.15pm Captain Jock Howitt, with a composite company (amongst whom was the writer of the journal) moved forward. The Battalion's history suggests that they had achieved their objective by 7.59 pm; the journal suggests that the attack was by no means as straightforward as that bald statement implies.

In any event, the line was pushed forward and established beyond the village. Some idea of the extent of the devastation can be gained from the fact that Captain Howitt was only able to identify the village from some heaps of bricks, which, 'after a bit of map reading', he decided were all that remained of the church. D Company appears to have been the first unit into Hollebeke and they then took up positions extending to the right of the village towards Forret Farm. Here they, along with B Company, held out for the next five days in appalling conditions. The rain had taken its toll on the support trenches and men up to their waists in mud and water struggled to bring up supplies to those in the front line. On one occasion a ration party was lost for 48 hours, and then turned up in the wrong part of the line. Even when the rations turned up they were often barely edible, being caked with mud through men falling into shell holes. The ground was not only a morass of mud and shell holes, it also reeked of gas, and as if these physical obstacles were not sufficiently daunting, the men also had to run the gauntlet of a continuous barrage from the enemy, determined to prevent supplies or guns coming forward. By 4 August (the third anniversary of the outbreak of war) the supply line, provided mostly by A and C Companies, was officially reported as being 'greatly depleted'.

It was only a matter of time before the Germans counter attacked, and this happened on the morning of 5 August. It seems as if the lookouts failed to keep a proper watch, and thus allowed German troops to infiltrate the British positions. Owing to heavy mist in the area, the SOS signals that were fired were not seen by headquarters, and reinforcements were not sent in time. In Hollebeke fierce hand-to-hand fighting took place, with the Company suffering heavy casualties, including Captain Howitt, who was killed in action less than a fortnight after being gazetted for the Military Cross. His body was later found surrounded by several enemy dead, and his name is now inscribed on the Menin Gate at Ypres. Both the author of the journal and his friend Private Williams were taken prisoner.

The narrative of the journal breaks off abruptly as the writer and his comrades are attempting to escape from the Germans. Captain Hector S. Walker, who took part in the action, which saw Hollebeke retaken, later described what happened next:

The mist suddenly lifted and we saw some of our men about to be marched off as prisoners. We shot the escort and released the prisoners. The mist kept lifting and falling again and completely obscured everything. Hollebeke was once more in our hands.

By noon both Forret Farm and Hollebeke had been retaken and the line re-established slightly forward of the positions held before the attack.

It emerged later that a group of two hundred storm troopers had been specially selected to carry out the surprise attack. When Hollebeke was retaken, it was found that D Company had been virtually wiped out. The writer of the journal and his friend Williams were very lucky to be alive. Private Wells was reported as missing, but it was later discovered that he had been killed, and, like Captain Howitt, his name can now be seen on the Menin Gate.

Casualties during this action were very high. From 24 July to 7 August they were as follows: killed, 23; died of wounds, 7; wounded, 115; missing, 54; sick (largely as a result of the terrible conditions in the trenches), 125; total: 324. Amongst the missing, over forty members of B and D Companies had been taken prisoner. Only ninety men of the Battalion remained, and they were pulled back out of the line, initially to Bois Confluent and then to Dezon camp, where it was possible to reorganize. Even then, however, their ordeal was not over, for on the 10th they were sent back to the front line near the White Chateau, suffering further casualties. Only on the evening of 13 August were they finally relieved, and on the following day the 'gallant remnants' returned to La Roukloshille. As Aston wrote later:

After these three terrible weeks rest was an absolute necessity. But the gaps in the Battalion were shocking: many a fine comrade had 'gone west', and their loss cast a gloom over the camp.

The writer of the journal tells that he was wounded in the leg, and presumably he was sent off to a field hospital and then to England. His friend Private Williams survived this action, but his luck ran out later in the year. The 12$^{th}$ East Surreys again formed part of the attacking force in the Battle of the Menin Road Ridge, which opened on 20 September 1917. Once again British troops were sent out in appalling conditions to attack a well-prepared enemy in strongly-defended positions. The men were under no illusions as to what was likely to happen. As Aston wrote later:

The old cheery spirit evident on other occasions when we were preparing to go into action was now absent. Rather was there an ominous silence. Hollebeke was too near to make one forget the awful times spent there. ... It was generally felt that we were up against something even worse than we had before experienced, and we were more concerned with what would be our ultimate fate than driving the enemy from the ridge.

Sadly, these forebodings were all too justified. Over the next four days, no fewer than 301 out of the 465 members of the Battalion who went into action became casualties, killed, wounded, or missing. Amongst these was Alfred Mark Williams. He was very badly wounded in the abdomen on the first day of the assault, was evacuated to a field hospital, and died there that evening at 10.45pm. He was nineteen years old. His grave can be found, along with two of his comrades, in the New Military Cemetery at Reninghelst, near Poperinghe.

No battalion could sustain casualties at this level and remain an effective fighting unit. On 28 September the 12th East Surreys were withdrawn from the front line and transferred to La Panne on the coast. There the Mayor of Bermondsey wrote to them:

> We in Bermondsey feel proud of the Boys; we were sure in the early days of the recruiting (when I personally did some work in this way) that the men of Bermondsey could be relied upon for their sterling fighting qualities, and they would do anything for those that led them well. The Battalion has been fortunate in its officers, and it has been a real pleasure to me to read from time to time of the many wonderful achievements performed by the whole of the men in your Brigade.

Aston's verdict on the action was predictably harsher. In his history of the Battalion he wrote:

> It was difficult not to weep then; it is hard to keep the tears back or restrain the pangs of sorrow and indignation in recalling it all now. But what is still more difficult to understand is why is not the united conscience of mankind mightily stirred till War—the stupidest, cruellest of all man's follies—is outlawed for ever?

1   R. Holmes, *Tommy: the British soldier on the Western Front, 1914–1918*
    (London, 2005), 631.

2   J. Aston and L. M. Duggan, *The History of the 12ᵗʰ (Bermondsey) Battalion,
    East Surrey Regiment* (London, 1936). All subsequent quotations are from
    this book.

3   These are held at the Surrey History Centre, Woking. The most useful
    in checking the details of *A Month at the Front* have been the Battalion's
    War Diary (7502/228) and Casualty List (7502/229).

*Who was the author of the journal?*

It has proved impossible so far to establish the identity of the author of *A Month at the Front.* However, he was unquestionably one of those wounded at Hollebeke on 5 August 1917. These were all listed in the Battalion's casualty list, which is now held, along with many of the other records of the Battalion, at the Surrey History Centre, Woking, and the following is a list of the eighteen privates reported as wounded on that day:

| | | |
|---|---|---|
| J. W. Carter | J. T. George | A. Manville |
| F. Clover | H. Gibbs | J. Millichamp |
| J. H. Cole | N. Haynes | H. M. Muspratt |
| R. Crowther | G. Kirby | S. Poulter |
| H. J. Gardner | G. Lincoln | A. Sargent |
| T. W. Gatford | A. Manley | A. Skinner |

Of these Crowther was wounded in the jaw, rather than leg, Gatford and George were killed later in the war, and Lincoln is mentioned by name in the journal, so our author is almost certainly one of the remaining fourteen. Any further information which would enable the Library to identify the author would be most welcome.

*John Pinfold*
February 2006

*Top:* Troops belonging to the 12<sup>th</sup> (Bermondsey) Battalion of the East Surrey Regiment in the Old French trench, June 1917

*Above:* The 'White Chateau', as photographed by the Germans, 1917.

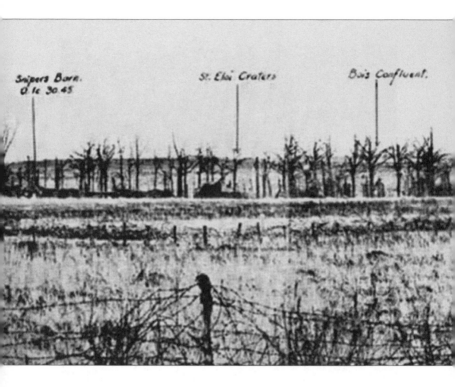

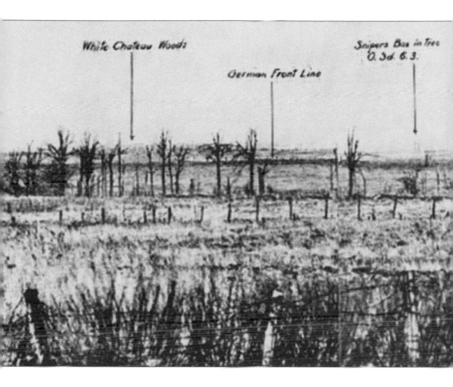

White Chateau Woods

German Front Line

Snipers Box in Tree
O. 3d. 6. 3.

View of the front, taken from St. Eloi, 1917. Several features
mentioned in the text are marked, including the Bois Confluent
and the White Chateau Woods.

Copy of Sister's Letter received on the 30-9-17.

Dear Mr.Williams,

         Your son Pte.Williams was brought into this hospital
yesterday very badly wounded in the abdomen.

         He was quite conscious on admission, but became gradually
worse and died at 10.45.p.m.

         He was very good and brave. He will be buried in an
English Cemetry, and his grave will be marked with a small wooden cross,
bearing his Name, No, and Regiment.

         All his personal belongings have been handed in, and you
will, I hope, receive them in due course. I am sorry to give you much
sad news of your son, but thought you would like to know how he died.

         With sincere sympathy,

               Yours very truly,

                      Sister J.B.Brotchie.


10th Corps.,

      Operating Centre,

           63rd Field Ambulance.

              B.E.F.


Regimental Address

        Pte.A.M.Williams,

        No. 240,508

        "D" Company,

           13th Platoon,

               12th East Surrey Regiment,

                    B.E.F.FRANCE


Buried at Reninghelst

        New Military Cemetry 2¼ miles S.W. Poperinghe.

------------------

Copy of the letter from Sister Brotchie of the 63<sup>rd</sup> Field Ambulance informing Private Williams' family of how he died. Such letters routinely stressed the bravery of those who had died, so that their families would not think they had died in vain or had suffered unduly.

*Above:* Photograph of Private Williams' grave in the Reninghelst Military Cemetery, as forwarded to his family by the War Office in 1917.

*Right:* Private Williams' grave with permanent headstone.

*Right:* Page from the Casualty List of the 12<sup>th</sup> East Surreys, showing the entries for some of those wounded in the action at Hollebeke on 5 August 1917 (Surrey History Centre, Woking, document 7502/229).

*Following page:* Part of the official account of the action at Hollebeke on 5 August 1917, as recorded in the daily War Diary of the 12<sup>th</sup> East Surreys (Surrey History Centre, Woking, document 7502/228).

| No. | Rank | Name | Initials | Remarks | Date |
|---|---|---|---|---|---|
| 4*34 | Pte | Elam | J. | | 6.8.17 |
| 5583 | " | Stacey | R.C. | | 4.8.17 |
| 6218 | " | Manley | H. | | 5.8.17 |
| 3756 | " | Lambert | C. | | 5.8.17 |
| 04548 | L/C | Pendred | E. | | 5.8.17 |
| 04348 | Pte | Rotherham | H.J. | | 5.8.17 |
| 31799 | " | Lincoln | S. | | 5.8.17 |
| 25539 | " | Kettle | G.W. | | 6.8.17 |
| 25551 | " | Stuspratt | H.M. | | 5.8.17 |
| 04399 | " | Cole | J.H. | | 5.8.17 |
| 3410 | " | Skinner | A. | | 5.8.17 |
| *864 | L/G | Miles | E.A. | | 5.8.17 |
| | 2/Lt | HAINE | R.M. | Set of duty | 31.7.17 |
| | 2/Lt | PALK | W.J. | Wd. Gas | 28.7.17 |
| 5355 | Pte | Gatford | A.W. | | 5.8.17 |
| 5342 | " | Bowes | W. | S.W.H.Rg. | 8.8.17 |
| 1283 | " | Gibbs | H | | 5.8.17 |
| 3757 | " | Ed Elven | J. | | 5.8.17 |
| 8371 | " | Manville | A. | | 5.8.17 |
| 6122 | Saj | Myers | A.S. | S W head | 5.8.17 |
| 6735 | Pte | Stebbings | J.W | Gas | 8.8.17 |
| 6058 | " | Elmer | J. | G.S.W. Elbow L | 10.8.17 |
| 1630 | " | Young | J. | S.W. Foot L. | 11.8.17 |
| 42210 | " | Crowther | R | G.S.W. Jaw | 5.8.17 |
| 25268 | " | Jago | W. | S.W. Thigh | 10.8.17 |
| 202463 | " | Coombes | A | | 12.8.17 |
| 25424 | " | Newman | A | . | 13.8.17 |
| 32687 | " | Plumbridge | H. | | 13.8.17 |
| 204781 | " | Watford | G.S. | | 13.8.17 |
| 25353 | " | Elliott | H. | | 13.8.17 |
| 25364 | " | Jones | J. | | 13.8.17 |
| 1032 | " | Brady | A | G.S.W. Eye thigh back | 13.8.17 |
| 25616 | " | Wood | A | | 13.8.17 |
| 5531 | " | Ives | H.P. | B Wd Scalp | 19.8.17 |

Instructions regarding War Diaries and Intelligence
Summaries are contained in F. S. Regs., Part II.
and the Staff Manual respectively. Title pages
will be prepared in manuscript.

W

INTELLIG

(Eras

| Place | Date | Hour | |
|-------|------|------|---|
| | 5. | | HOLLEBEKE and advancing on OPTIC T |
| | | | was sent up from our H.Q. + a runn |
| | | | The mist was still heavy d our |
| | | | turned out + advanced towards HOLLEB |
| | | | SUPPORT LINE a continued to advance |
| | | | held up by enemy M. G. fire + Snip |
| | | | their line whom we made prisoners |
| | | | English + we were unable to ascerta |
| | | | of the enemy attacking. We were now |
| | | | who had occupied dugouts on the le |
| | | | but was unable to get into touch |
| | | | + Snipers. A few Germans were as |
| | | | who had come forward as they appro |
| | | | was in command |
| | | | sent forward a strong fighting patro |
| | | | The whole line was then pushed |
| | | | the line we held prior to the at |
| | | | of the EAST SURREYS (about 25 c |
| | | | + "B" Coys: the mist being so |
| | | | they could give any alarm. In |
| | | | BOIS CONFLUENT, but the deta |
| | | | Company |
| | | | Platoon   of a Composite  formed |

SUMMARY.

(required.)

| Events and Information | Remarks and references to Appendices |
|---|---|

...ll our lines from Battn. H.Q. were "dis." This S.O.S.
...ed to the HANTS REGT. H.Q. & to Brigade H.Q.
...s not seen. Under Major Pennell the H.Q. Coy.
...joined up with a Coy. of the HANTS. REG. in NEW
...about 200 yds. of HOLLEBEKE where we were
...encountered a few Germans who were forward of
...was asserted that they could not speak French or
...them any information as to the numbers or location
...with another Coy. of the HANTS. Regt. on our left
...LLEBEKE. A patrol went out on the right
...her troops. This patrol was fired on by enemy M.G.
...retreating. They were probably enemy patrols
...isolated from their main body. Major Pennell who
...LLEBEKE was reported to be clear of the enemy.
...a positions were established slightly forward of
...HOLLEBEKE. Lt. PRIDHAM then took command
...s appear to have lost many prisoners in "D"
...inarily, heavy our posts were surrounded before
...ning the Battn. (about 90 strong) moved to
...r Capt. OPPENSHAW moved up the line as a
...h Regt. in the Brigade. Figures are unobtainable

## PROLOGUE

The events recorded in this book relate to the time the writer was actively engaged 'Up the Line', and do not include any 'happenings' which occurred during his time of 'Preparation' or 'Waiting' behind the lines.

N.B. *Actual dates cannot be given as the writer cannot remember them accurately.*

It was as near as I can remember, about the middle of July 1917, that the ('D' boy, 12th East Surreys) were ordered 'up the line', which meant we were to move up and take up our positions in some support trenches. We understood we were to hold these for about six days, and then return for a few days' rest.

We marched off from our billets one morning, and in due time arrived at a pleasant little spot in a little wood, and there had our dinner, and rested for the night. Now, before I proceed further, I may as well say that at this particular spot we were 'sorted out' a bit, or inspected, to see that everything was in perfect order for 'Activities'. This took place on the following day, as there were several defects and deficiencies, we had to stay the following night, so we had two nights rest. A few men (there are always some on these occasions) managed to get bad feet, or bad legs, or some other complaint they had never had before, so they were left here for other duty, when the rest of us marched off next morning. One of these men had been in my personal company for quite a long time, and I had hopes of his coming to the Front with me, but now I discovered him to be what I call a 'Shirker'. It is a surprising fact that many of these can be found at the Front.

In due time (late in the afternoon) we arrived at the

entrance track, or rough roadway, along which we were to go in order to get to our trenches. We halted for some considerable time, and enjoyed the rest, for we were all very tired.

By this time, I had made my first acquaintance with Heavy Gun Fire (Field Guns I mean), for we had passed close by one or two monsters close to the road, and when they fired we were almost blown down. At last we were ordered to 'Fall in' and very soon we came to the first shell holes I had ever seen, Battlefield shell holes, I mean. There were plenty of empty shell cases lying about too, and now and then an unexploded one. I was greatly interested in all this, and as the shell holes did not appear to be newly made, I thought they were <u>Old ones</u>, and walked down the road quite comfortable, never dreaming that horses and men tore up and down that road at top speed, for Dear life sometimes. I discovered this afterwards.

We went down this road for about half a mile and could see our trenches over to the right, so we branched off in single file over the broken ground, and soon got into our place, the other regiment coming out, and I had a decent dug out, half circular in shape, thus,

and I had four other fellows to share it with. Their names were Brown, Whiting, Watts and another fellow whose name I forget.

Brown was a young fellow, merry and bright, but who

always used filthy language. He had been a professional pugilist before the war.

Whiting was an older man, quiet and respectable, and swore very little. He had been 'up to the Front before', so I told him I should look to him for advice if I wanted it.

Watts was a young fellow, with a very active tongue, and used filthy talk at times. The other fellow was young, quiet, and sulky.

Just outside were two other chums of mine (I call them chums because we used to live in the same trench), Sabin and Lincoln. Sabin was appointed Stretcher bearer as soon as we got settled.

I had now time to have a look round, and I noticed that at our backs, at about 500 yards distant, were several British Guns in action, of course, and the shells they fired over our heads. The noise in the air sometimes was terrific, being like a lot of express trains rushing by. There were other guns on our left, big ones too, for the earth used to rock when they fired. Between us and these Guns was a road.

It was now evening and I noticed that some German Shells were falling with a horrible crash near our Guns. These shells also came over our heads, and we could always hear them coming. They soon came in large numbers and began to drop near the road, and a little later our trench came in for a fair share. I concluded by that the Germans had evidently got the range of our guns, the road, and our trench.

Now, along this road, a lot of traffic passed especially in the evening, and at night, Red Cross vans, motor lorries, men, horses, water carts, ammunition carts, and guns, and often in the middle of the night 'Caterpillar Engines' would sneak up with a huge gun, which in the morning would be giving the Germans 'beans' or rather, some big shells.

It never mattered how fast the shells fell, there was always this traffic up and down this road, it never ceased. I used to watch it by daylight and sad sights met my eyes occasionally.

One evening a party of horse soldiers was going up, and a large shell dropped among them and three of their horses bolted off riderless. The poor riders were picked up later by Stretcher Bearers. Very often when we looked out of a morning we saw an overturned ration cart, or a dead horse, or a van lying by the side of the road. After what I saw, I thought we were tremendously lucky in getting in as we did. The first night passed unevently, except that we were shelled. The second evening came, and rumours went round that there was to be a working party that night. What the work was nobody knew, but we were to go to Head Quarters first. About 50 of us had to turn out, and we started at 10 o'clock. Our Lieutenant leading, we picked our way in single file over the shell holes, and got into the road. What a journey we had that night, it was enough to turn anyone's hair grey. Shells of course were falling all the time, some of them quite close enough to be uncomfortable. After going up this awful road about half a mile, we turned off on a side track, and later on the rough ground again. Every now and then we would stop and then turn in another direction. I now concluded that our leader had lost the way, which unfortunately proved to be the case. Backwards and forwards we went, over shell holes, sometimes over a railway track, sometimes over a road, and once or twice we got into our own batteries of guns. The din was awful, and the blast from the Guns almost knocked us down. We continued floundering about for a long time, but at last got to the right place. To our surprise, our Officer, after making enquiries said 'There is no working party tonight, boys, so we are now going home'.

(We were really too late for work.)

After a long walk we arrived 'Home' in the early hour of the morning. Another working party was formed (from the rest of our company) for the next day, and their work consisted of carrying bombs and ammunition from Headquarters, to a dump further up. They all returned 'Home' safely, but said they had had a very warm time. I went off again the following evening with another working party to carry up more Ammunition. We started about eight o'clock, when the shelling was very thick, but as it was still daylight, we did not miss our way. We kept to the road all the time and way to Head Quarters and had a very exciting time altogether. While going down the road a huge shell fell only a few feet way from me, but it never exploded! If it had done, you would not have been reading this book. Once or twice we ran for dear life, but managed to reach Head Quarters safe and sound. After a few minutes rest here, we we[re] ordered off to the Ammunition Depot at the Royal Engineers Quarters further up, and arriving here we had to wait quite a long time, so we sat down on boxes of bombs at the side of the road. Off we went and very soon had to get into a trench for safety. This trench led across a large open space (all shell holes) up to <u>Battle Wood</u>, and we had a perilous journey across here, often having to stop on account of Gas shells. At last we reached the Wood and got out of the trench. This wood is a most awful place, it is full of trees standing, it is also full of fallen trees, and shells from German Guns sweep through here constantly. The ground is strewn with limbs of trees and trunks of trees, and is full of shell holes, and is a veritable death trap. It requires some nerve to go through this wood. It is only about 500 yards through this wood, but it took us nearly half an hour to go through it. Right in the middle of the wood is a pile of white stones which is all that remained of 'White Chateau'.

Having got through this we were once again in open country, and toddled on a little further and reached our destination, and also returned 'Home' safely, but as usual very tired.

Then next afternoon I was on another party, this time to go down to Head Quarters and bring back some ammunition to our own trench. I have only one item of interest to record about this, I had a very narrow escape, when I had nearly reached 'Home'. The Enemy were shelling us with high explosives, viz shells, that burst in the Air and scatter a shower of bullets down on you, and I and another boy, who was helping me to carry a box of bombs, had just arrived at the Cemetery at the top part of the field, where our own trenches are, when a shell burst over our heads, and a shower of Bullets flew around us, and several fell, quite close to my feet (within two inches in fact). This made us hurry up, although I had a very anxious time with my boy, as he had bad feet and could not get along. However, we all reached home safe and sound. One fellow had a bullet strike his steel helmet, and make a great dent in it, but luckily it did not touch his head. At other times I often went across to the road to fetch up our rations from the Ration Cart. This was anything but a pleasant journey sometimes, as we often had to dodge shells. Then we had to fetch our own drinking water. No water cart ever came up to us, the East-Surreys, so we had to go with two petrol cans each, up this awful road in parties of 20. We had to fetch the water from an old building, about three quarters of a mile away, and I am glad to say we were always successful in getting home safely. One night we were experiencing an unusually heavy shelling, and it became so hot that our Officers actually 'got wind up' (a very common expression out there for being timid or frightened) and about midnight we were to dress and stand ready for moving off at a moments notice. Nothing happened however, and after a time the shelling cooled down and we were ordered to bed again. I could not see where we were going, if we did move off, for to advance or retire in that awful shell fire would mean certain death to many of us, and I thought it was madness even to think of such a thing. It was bad enough to stay there, and to move on would be ten times worse. The Hampshires were just below us in the same trench, and in the morning when we turned out we discovered that a shell had gone right into one of the dugouts and killed nine of the poor fellows. We saw them brought out the same day and they were buried up in the Cemetery at the top. A sad sight, I can assure you and one which made us think.

On another occasion I went with another party in the afternoon to dig a trench at the far end of the <u>Battle Wood</u>. We reached the place safely and commenced our task, which was just in the wood. Shells as usual screamed through the trees, but we dug on. We witnessed an Air fight from here. There was a regular swarm of hostile Aircraft overhead and a few British ones. We could hear them fire their machine guns at each other, and presently two of them got out by themselves. We watched these two firing at each other for some little time, when down came the British machine. The German had got the better of him. I have seen ever so many encounters, but never yet have I seen the British get up so high as the enemy or an enemy machine brought down. We then continued our digging but the shells troubled us so much that we were ordered into the West Kent Head Quarters for safety. We had to shelter so long that when the shelling cooled off it was time for us to return which we did in safety. I might mention that during these journeys to and fro it was nothing unusual to come across a dead horse sometimes two with great holes in their sides caused by shells, and now and then a dead Comrade would be lying waiting for burial. Sometimes we saw them 'knocked out'. Sad sights, but it was War. Sometimes when we were on our homeward journey we would find the road blown up in many places, but it did not matter, as it would be immediately repaired. This particular road leading to Head Quarters was made of planks (oak) four or five inches thick and these often were splintered to smithereens. It was from the lower edge of Battle Wood, that I saw the famous Hill 60 where so many of our Brave Lads laid down there lives, I don't wonder at it either, and I realized, that with the enemy on that Hill it must have been a terrible task to dislodge him. I stood watching it one day and wondered where poor Edgar Springer fell, it was undoubtedly somewhere close to where I was standing. (He was in the East Surrey's too). I wondered if he was buried in the Cemetery just outside, but I never had time to look in any of them. No other event of special importance occurred while at this support trench. There were two nights when I preferred to sleep outside of my dug out, because the shelling made it rock so much, and as I was in at the far end, I had no wish the be suffocated or buried if a shell should knock it down. We had to wash in dirty stinking water all the time we were here, as there was no other water about excepting that which half filled the shell holes. Time went on and we began to wonder when we should get relief. Our six days passed and our seventh arrived. It was on this day I believe that the news went around that we were to go up the First line trench for about six hours, it would not in any case be more than ten hours and then we were to be relieved for certain. Several more days passed and we were not moved up and I began to wish we did make a move soon, as every day the shelling on our trench became more violent. At last, however the order came for us to move up, and we cleared out of it and in due time arrived in our new trench, but as usual tired and still thinking that relief would come soon.

We spent the first night comparatively quiet, and the next day passed unevently except for the usual shell fire. Orders had come up that an advance was to be made and the West Kents and the Kings Royal Rifles were going over the top, and as soon as they had reached their objective we should be relieved. We were to advance to the enemy trenches 20 minutes after the West Kents and the Kings Royal rifles had left. We were to hold this trench until relief came. Well I thought this was coming a bit thick, tired troops to go over and hold newly taken trenches. But still it was very characteristic of the East Surrey's. The British 'Barrage' was to start at a given time and after 4 hours of that over the top for the West Kents and the Kings Royal Rifles. I had no idea when this Barrage was to begin, but early the next morning I was greatly started by it. The screaming of the shells and report of the guns just behind us was too awful. I thought it was German Aeroplanes bombing us overhead but no, it was our Barrage. I soon got used to it and soon saw our particular Aeroplane coming and going and signaling to the Gunners as to how things were. The time passed and the Barrage eased but we had to stay till late in the afternoon.

We had a First Aid Station at the end of our trench and the wounded kept coming in all day and it had now begun to rain, which made it very miserable for us. Some of us had to take a turn at stretcher bearer taking bad cases from our trench across the open country at the back down to the West Kents Head Quarters at Battle Wood. A perilous job that was. I did not have to go myself, for, as I was waiting, orders came that we were to get over to the next front trench at once, so away we went. We had to take a spade each, as we were to go forward into 'no mans land' and dig ourselves in. Now we understood that the West Kents and the Kings Royal Rifles had failed to reach their objective (The German third line, so the East Surreys were to do it, yes, always the East Surreys if there was any finishing off to do, yes the East Surreys would go through even with worn and tired out troops, if any regiment went short of food it would be the East Surreys always). It appeared that the enemy had got too many machine guns to allow their 3rd lines to be taken so we were to work around a bit and attack in a different direction. We got over the front trench safely and here we waited for some considerable time, being re-organized and told off in our respective parties, viz machine gunners, followed by bombers and rifle grenadiers, the riflemen were to be well ahead of all the rest so we formed up and waited the order to start off. At last it came and we started out into that piece of land which lies between the British and German trenches and which is known as 'no mans land', and is rightly named too. We made our way through mud and slush up to our knees in places and it was such a struggle that some of the men through away their spades (they were fools to do this and the N.C.O's) ought to have stopped them). We soon came to what had been the enemies Front Line and of course we saw plenty of dead Germans lying about. What a sight it was The British Barrage had played terrible havoc with them. We passed on and noticed in front of us a huge pile of bricks and rubbish and from this a German sniper began to worry us.

It was necessary therefore to hunt him up before we could continue our journey in peace, so we immediately began to try and spot him, no easy job as a sniper is a picked man and knows how to keep under cover. We pushed on a little further and halted, this is where we were to dig in. It was now late in the evening but quite light. We could see the Germans in front of us only about 300 yards difference and of course they could see us. I thought it was a very foolish piece of business ever to come down there in the open in broad daylight to dig in, but it is just like the British Army more especially the East Surreys. We started digging and of course shells began to drop near us. It wasn't likely the Germans were going to let us dig in there without giving us a warm reception. Now, as I said before many of the men had thrown away their spades and they had to use their entrenching tools which was absolutely useless for rapid work so many of them were exposed to the fire longer than the others. I had my spade and lost no time in getting into the earth. Our Corporal was working next to me and the shelling was so terrible that I said to him, 'We shall never get out of this Corporal' he said 'Oh yes we shall you are alright'. I did not think any of us would be alive in the morning, neither did the Corporal because one of the Sergeants came along to him a little later and I overheard their conversation. The Sergeant said 'it was suicide' and we should all soon be killed and so on, very pleasant, wasn't it. However we stuck it and I soon got down deep enough to get temporary cover, so I handed over my spade to someone else. We had a most awful night but did not suffer any casualties. We finished off our trench the next day, near enough to provide us with a certain amount of protection. It was very wet, however and it soon became so muddy that we were kept employed in chucking it out. At my end it was so soft, that we sank in nearly to our knees and as we could not keep it cleared we had to make the best of it. We got into a pretty state altogether, mud all over our equipment, mud all over our rifles and mud over everything. Our N.C.O's had left us to it and had gone into a dugout and there they stayed for the rest of the time so far as the rest of the trench were concerned. The Sergeant came round once a day with a ration of rum, a teaspoonful seemed to be sufficient for the East Surrey for that is the quantity we each had. I was very interested in watching the Germans, they had been pestering our fellows as usual, but they had been spotted and they were making for home as fast as they could, taking refuge behind a tree, but every time they got in sight we could hear a report of a rifle. I saw two of them fall in the field as they were running at full speed and I believe a third fell among the trees. Anyway it so scared the rest they didn't do any more sniping while I was there. Now we had been in our trench for several days and nights and as usual no relief was coming, so one by one the fellows left the trench and went into various dug outs for a rest. Personally I didn't like these dug outs as they were so often under heavy shell fire and sometimes when one had gone in there he had to stay till it was possible to get out. There was a big one just behind us and only 20 yards off. From this down to our trench was all that remained of a hedge, but it afforded us just a little covering while we went to and fro. A terrible perilous journey it used to be for some of our fellows, although only 20 yards. They would be shelled and often had to run to get in. I used to go up and down there and not once was I fired on. I bore a charmed life it seemed for I was never touched. I used to use my brains and choose my time to get out and in, I used to study this shelling business, and my judgements usually proved correct. I never went into this dug out because I did not think it safe. It was a big place made of concrete and steel and was about 12 feet by 7 and about a foot thick. It was already perched up on end at an angle of 45 degrees. The British Gunners had done this when driving the enemy out, but it afforded good shelter, our fellows thought, so they took possession. I never had any rest however accept when I sat down in a muddy trench and dozed off for 10 minutes or quarter of an hour. I was now left in my particular trench with four men and I began to get a bit ruffled as I did not think it fair that we should have it all to do, and I made up my mind to strike in the morning regardless of consequences. We had nothing to do eat and also nothing to drink (I find my memory has led me on too fast as I have omitted one or two details). It was about the second night I think that a certain Corporal while strolling around about midnight discovered and caught a German in our lines. I knew this sort of thing would be going on, unless we kept a sharp look out no doubt some of our sleepy headed fellows had let him through. He was brought down to where I was and it was decided to let Sergeant Critton take him over to Head Quarters. He started on this mission but whether he ever got his prisoner through or not nobody seemed to know, as Sergeant Critton was never seen again in our quarters. A little later on another prisoner was captured by the same Corporal and he likewise was sent off in charge of another Corporal, that Corporal was never seen again in our quarters, a little later on again, a third prisoner was brought down to Corporal Sewell, my Corporal next to me. They stood arguing who should take him down Corporal Sewell did not know the way and did not want to go either. The other could not take him as he had to keep a look out, so they decided to leave him in our trench under Sewell's care. We had him in and he sat down between Sewell and myself. I immediately searched him and asked him if he had any knives about him. He put his hands up and made me understand he had nothing whatever except his smoke helmet. Even this I made him open so that I could look inside. I would run no risks, if the other fellows did. He had nothing harmful about him so I began to question him as to how many mates he had with him and where they were etc. He told me there were four others out there, indicating the direction, so search was made, but they had evidently made off for we didn't find them and no more troubled us that night. We kept the Prisoner in our trench for an hour or more, and then Cpl Sewell thought he had better go off with him, so he went. Well I thought this is a nice state of things and very foolish too, to go off with Prisoners single handed in the middle of the night. Now I know what I should have done if I had captured them, I should have marched straight up to the nearest dug out, where about a dozen of our men were resting and said, 'Here you are chaps, look after this prisoner till the morning.' and then hand him over to the Sergeant, that is what I should have done with all three. My Private opinions and suggestions I kept to myself. It didn't do to say too much, besides I was only a Private. Well I thought, someone would have to suffer for it, sooner or later and sure enough they did, for the order came round in the morning <u>no</u> man was to leave the trenches, so that meant I should have to stay in the trench for still longer and I thought it very hard. We stuck it (the few of us who were left) all the next day. Now, I had a chap next to me in the Corporal's place (I might mention here that Cpl Sewell did not come back.) who I shall describe as a fool, for fool he was for certain. Well, night came, and when it was getting dark one of the officers came round to us and said, 'Who is in this trench.' I answered 'I was' and he said 'How many others have your with you,' I said four. Well he said 'do you know it is very important that you should have a sentry at night,' I said, Yes, I know that, then he said 'You must take it in turns' Very well sir', so I took first turn about 10-o-clock. I always have my eyes skinned at night all the time I was in the trench, woe betide any Germans who got in front of my rifle while I was on the look out. About 11-30 I aroused on of my mates and told him to keep a sharp look out, so he took his turn. He stood up looking over the Parapet for about five minutes and then he dropped off to sleep. I knew this would happen with all of them in turn for they were so sleepy. I was sleepy too just as much as they, and quite as tired, but I wasn't going to sleep with such danger lurking round. I kept knocking first one and then the other to keep them awake and sat down in the trench while they <u>were</u> awake. The night passed in this fashion and in the morning they wanted something to eat, so two or three of them went up to the dugouts to see if there were any rations about. They came back later on and said the Sgt. would send something down shortly, he did so, we had bread and jam and mud but no drink. Now another little incident occurred which ruffled me, I noticed two or three Germans at the bottom of the field were very busy doing something outside their dugout and facing us. I wondered what they were up to, and soon discovered they were putting up a machine gun. They ought to have been stopped at once, it could easily have been done. About two shells from our Artillery would have blown the place to pieces, but no, they were allowed to fix up in front of our eyes, and I knew we should have to suffer for it, sure enough we did too. That very evening the Captain had about a dozen men out in the open not far from the dug out near me and was giving them certain orders when this deadly machine gun began to play on them. Before they could get to the dug out two of them were killed outright and several wounded including Whiting the quiet man who had been in the trench with me. Watts I never saw again, nor the other fellow whose name I forgot. I now arrive at the time when I was left with the four men in the trench. These four men were with me for the night. Well night arrived and I did a turn at 'Sentry' and got the fool to do his turn, but after that I did the whole thing right through the night I got so sick of trying to keep the other fellows awake that I gave it up in disgust. Now in the night the fool was sitting on a plank of earth which separated us from the adjoining trench and was nodding off to sleep as usual, when I shouted Ford (his name) if you fall asleep there and fall backward into that mud you know what the consequences will be, don't you. He muttered yes, and later after he had had a narrow escape he turned round, so had his feet in it. Well in the morning he was so deep in that I actually had to dig him out. I wasn't very complimentary about it either while I was doing it. I certainly did let him have it and I told him to clear out of it, which he soon did, the other also went to see if there was any food about. They did not come back so I had the whole length of the trench to myself. Now I thought I can make the trench more comfortable I started making it deeper and wider and in the middle of the afternoon a party of machine gunners came up and immediately began to fix up a machine gun close to my trench and just at my back. Well, I thought, here is another piece of fine work, come down here in broad daylight and fix up a gun with the enemy looking on. Well, the Germans soon began to shell them with Whiz Bangs, a shell that skims along instead of dropping straight down, awful things when close. This shelling became so hot that they could not put up with it so they got into my trench. Well I thought this is worse still for me, for I was sure the enemy would see them getting into my trench I expect they did too, for the shells began to pepper along close to us. I experienced an awful $\frac{1}{4}$ hour there with those men. Never do I want to go under such another ordeal. The shells were exploding quite close to the edge of our trench, and mud and dirt flew in all directions. I was expecting every moment to have a shell in the trench. It was lucky for me I had deepened the trench for if I hadn't our heads would have been blown off. As it was one shell came right through one side of the trench and out the other. This was only two inches above my head and I was stooping down at the time. Another one followed almost as close, and I thought it was time to clear out so I told the machine gunners to get out of it, I could not get out before they did. So they did so, and so did I. I noticed all the others that were adjoining the trenches had also gone. I made my way as fast as I could towards a dug out, not with the intention of going into it, but I thought I might as well take refuge behind one of those places for the time being, and I had just got up within a couple of yards when a shell crashed into it and exploded with terrific force, blinding me for a few minutes and killing two of my mates inside, and wounding several others. Their cries were terrible to hear as I went past. This shell I might mention must have passed very close to me, in fact it must almost have touched me. I stumbled on over bricks and stones through shell holes, and others joined me, and we laid down behind a huge mass of bricks etc, which was another dug out. The Germans were intent on driving us out of it however for they began to pepper this with big shells, we could not stay there, so cleared off to another, neither could we stay here for the shells began to drop there also, I could plainly see the Germans had spotted us running about in a party, so I decided to go off by myself. I wandered about looking for shelter and hardly knew where to go. I looked at one place then at another, but they would not do, so I came to a huge piece of concrete which I thought would hide me for a time. It was really the dug out that was struck by a shell only I did not know it, as I had approached it from another direction. I looked at it and thought, well it might be alright, but I did not like to risk it, and looking ahead I saw a trench and a man I knew getting into it, I stumbled down to him and he said, 'Where are you off to' I answered into this trench, he said 'Look sharp about it or you'll get sniped'. I got in close to him but he was in a part to himself. I mean there was a division between us, we started chatting about the event we had just gone through and so on. As yet I could not make out where we were so I asked him and to my great surprise I discovered it was the very trench out of which we were about half an hour ago, in fact my own trench. It was some time before I could realize it, but it was so I approached it from another direction and the shells had altered the surface a bit and I was so shaken up that I did not recognise it at first, no one will ever realize what it is to be driven about as we were that afternoon. It was something awful and no words will ever [be able] to describe my feelings accurately. Well there were no shells to speak of about now so I thought I would dig myself in deeper and cut a shelter in the side of it so I set to work. I hadn't been there long when the Sgt came down with the rum and gave me a drop, not a big drop either, so when he had finished with the man next to me, I asked him for another drop which he gave me, not without a little murmur. Oh no, I continued my digging and later on another fellow came and joined Wells the man next to me so we three kept company by chatting over the top.

Presently Williams (this new chap) said he was going to find us something to eat, so off he went and came back with plenty of bread and several tins of jam. He threw me a whole tin of jam and gave me some bread and now I thought I really would have some jam, as five or six of us usually had to share a tin of this size. I tucked into it and laid it on thick and enjoyed myself for a little while. When I had nearly emptied the tin I thought it would be polite to ask if anyone else was to have it so I asked 'Williams' and he said 'No' so I finished it off and threw the tin over the top, thoroughly satisfied to get such a meal. I resumed my digging and just before dark the Captain came round and had a look into my trench and said 'that's all right you'll be safe in there, that's very good'. He went off without saying anything further and I wondered what was coming off next. The Sgt came round afterwards and said they were going out on a raid that night, and the machine gunners were to be a their posts to keep the enemy from running up this way. He also said he would see if he could get 'Us Chaps' relieved presently, but I didn't expect it now. I then began considering my position I had to stay in that trench, alone, and would have to stand against a German Barrage fire which would be the case when the raid started. I concluded that would finish me up, so far as this world was concerned. However, as the Raiders were about to start off, word came that every man was to leave the trench and go into the dug outs for shelter. This we did, Williams coming in with me, and Wells into another place where some of the others were. My dug out was a fairly strong one being built of bricks, concrete and steel girders. It was originally in the German hands and it was now occupied by about 10 of us altogether. It was full of water at the bottom and to get to our seats we had to wade into water which was up to our knees in the deepest part. For three days and three nights we sat in that dug out with our feet dangling in water and twice we had to bale out some of it, as it kept rising. My seat was a box of German bombs. I thought at first it might be a case of bottled beer or whisky and I got a bayonet and opened it and found to my disappointment it was a box of bombs. This I even had to raise up occasionally or I should have been sitting in water. Even in this dug out we weren't without excitement, one night our guard saw two men whom he took to be Germans walking about, and so we were soon on the alert with our rifles in our hands and standing in the water all ready to rush out at once if necessary. There were two men and they came up to us, but it was not light enough to see if they were the enemy or our own fellows. We could see others, too, creeping about in the open and concluded a German raiding party was about to raid us. Shells were falling thick and fast (they always were). We were never free from this horrid shell fire and we thought the best thing to do was to keep quiet at least for a time. For an hour we stood there watching and we fancied we could see them creeping up, I said, we must not let them get close enough to throw a bomb inside here or we are done for. The best thing we can do is to wait until they are nearly close enough and then run out with a yell and fire rapidly and they will think there is quite a lot of us, and probably make off. Nothing came of it however and the shaddows moved off, and in the morning as soon as it was light enough we discovered that a good many of these Germans were nothing more than a few short willow shrubs waving about in the breeze. We had a good laugh but they had given us a fright. There were of course two or three real bodies about as Headquarters was only a few yards from us and we had seen several go in there. But they were of course our own men. Nothing else of any importance happened there till the fight began. We each took our turn at guard or sentry outside, a hot job at times especially when machine guns were on us. Deadly things these were and I had a horrible dread of them. We had our meals regularly and had a tot of rum each day. This tot was half a mug between five. For drink, we had water from a shell hole just outside. We selected this hole as being the cleanest one and reserved it for drinking purposes only. It had a very peculiar taste, I don't know quite what it tasted like, but we had to drink a certain amount of it as there was nothing else. There may have been a dead German lying at the bottom of it for all we knew. There were more unlikely things than that, especially in this spot. The Sgt used to tell us when he came with our rum that relief was coming tonight or tomorrow but it never came. The last time he came in he said relief was coming tomorrow for certain. I had made up my mind to have my relief tomorrow shells or no shells. I was intending to go down to the doctor and have my feet seen to. They were in a bad state through being in water so long. We had orders that night to form up outside in a certain order and we did that, and we were told that was exactly what we were to do should there be a counter attack. I concluded by this that the officers were evidently expecting something to happen but we retired into our dug outs once more and took our rest. At about 4 o'clock the next morning we were ordered to stand to, we clambered out and discovered the enemy close on us in fact they were so close that we could not form up at all. The din and confusion were something awful and we scattered immediately, some one way and some another. Bullets were flying in all directions and shells were dropping all over the place and it is a marvel to me that we were able to get out of it as we did. I, with four or five comrades rushed round by the back of our dug out and I had only gone a few yards when a shell burst just behind me, knocked me down flat on my face in the mud, I struggled up and went on through the awful mud and caught up my mates who were now halting and having a look round. An officer had joined them too so I thought we should now be alright. He said 'Hang together boys' and started of again, we following. We went on for some time struggling over shells holes often up to our knees in mud and now we had reached a barbed wire entanglement. This we scrambled through and went on for a bit further when we again halted and had a look round to take our bearings. Dawn was now breaking and we could see a little better and looking to our right we discovered we were close on top of a large body of men who were advancing. I had only three chums left with me and the officer on seeing these Germans flew off for all he was worth and was soon out of sight. I shall never forget him or respect him either for rushing off and leaving us to our fate. Of course he had no equipment so he stood more chance than we did. If he only said 'Goodbye lads' when he left us I should have thought more of him, but he had properly got the wind up and left us without saying a word. The Germans had spotted us and with a yell several of them made for us. They were quite close and in trying to get away I stumbled into a shell hole and gave myself up for lost. I saw one German who had his eye on me, preparing to throw a hand grenade at me. I was now lying on my back and facing my opponent and saw him going to hit me right enough. I turned over on my chest so as to receive it on my back. This, I thought is the end, so far as I am concerned. The Grenade struck me on the lower part of my back and exploded, and beyond giving me a big push into the mud did me no harm. I looked over my shoulder and saw my oponent about to throw another at me, which he did immediately. This also was a straight aim. I received it higher on my back, and like the other did me no harm except give me a shock. Where the fragments of the sheet cases went to I don't know and it was only providence that kept them out of my body. My oponent had now come up and several others and I saw my escape was impossible. Now, I could have shot my Captor and several others with my rifle before they had time to come up to me if I had chosen but I quickly decided the Germans would undoubtedly kill me without mercy and my mates as well, so, as my oponent arrived on the scene I threw up my hands and surrendered. My Chums I noticed were still trying to escape, but as I saw they were surrounded, I shouted, 'Chuck it', and they chucked. Now during this time it was really all over in a few minutes. I never lost my nerve and even when on various occasions I gave myself up for lost and thought the end had come, I was quite prepared to die calmly. I got up out of that shell hole and felt quite comfortable, I was greatly interested in these Germans, it was a new sight for me, so I took stock of my Captors for private reasons of my own in view of future events. I was a P.O.W. but I never intended going to Germany not me, there would be some rough work before I reached that notorious country. One of my chums Williams was a very quick witted chap, and I knew he would understand a nod and a wink from me, so I had not yet given up hopes of escape. We threw off all our equipment and handed over our rifles and knives and three Germans were told off to march us away to their Headquarters, I presumed. These three fellows were very decent chaps and gave us a drink form their coffee bottles and treated us much better than I expected. We started off and I noticed my Chums had stuck to their Gas helmets but I had forgotten mine. I was a fool for doing this, for if a gas cloud came along I should be a dead man, however no gas of any sort troubled us, so I did not have the bother of a helmet and I was not such a fool as I thought. We were marched along in single file, one German in front leading, I was next, my chums behind me and the other two Germans in the rear. Sometimes we had to hurry up and run for a little while and we continued our journey like this for some time. My brain worked all the time I was doing that journey if ever it did. I looked up at my Captor in front and thought, How easily I could have you over on your back, that I could and disarm you. Yes I boast I could, but it was the two beggars in the rear who would want reckoning with. For the time I must dismiss all thought of this so we still toddled on. Now I began to notice our Captors were a little doubtful about the direction and halted once or twice and had a look round. We continued on however and presently in front of us I saw a hedge, I saw a rifle fired through, my leading German was shot through the shoulder and fell to the ground shouting Kamerad, Kamerad, I received a wound in the leg at the same time and fell into a shell hole, while the others took refuge in another. Shells were now falling thick and fast and the machine guns began to sweep the ground. The shelling increased and we were now experiencing a terrible time. I was half covered with muddy water and my leg pained me terribly, and I considered my shell hole was none too deep for me to feel comfortable, as one side of it was broken away and this allowed my head to be partly exposed in one direction. As the shells skimmed along just above my head and machine gun bullets began to strike the earth on the opposite side I decided I must get myself down further into the water and began to scoop away the mud and slush with my hands, and pile it up in front of my head to screen it from view. I endured the most awful agony in that shell hole, what with the pain in my leg and the thoughts, sad some of them were, that flashed though my brain, and the groaning of the wounded Germans at the top and the screech and explosions of the shells, it was awful. No words will ever describe the horror of it all. I wondered what my dear wife would do when I was gone, for I never expected to get out of that hole alive and many other thoughts crossed my mind.